Foreword

Watching the images on the news of NHS staff working long
hours under terrific pressure, risking and losing their lives to
help the British people, we felt pretty useless messing about
on a Friday night cooking on an internet meeting.

But then realised we were already doing something
useful.....staying at home, and not adding to the problem.

This book is dedicated to all the NHS staff who risked and
lost their lives helping the British people through the Covid
19 pandemic.

Contents

Mains

Some Desserts

A couple of cakes

Two Strong Cocktails

Mains

Deny's Fish Curry
This was where it all began, the first demo from our groovy Man from Mauritius!

Ingredients - Serves 2
2 tbsp Madras curry powder
1 tbsp Tomato purée
3 Curry leaves
1 tsp ground cumin
1 tsp Turmeric
4 cloves of garlic crushed
5cm of fresh ginger finely chopped
1 White onion
Aubergine cut into small cubes
Fish of your choice (a firm fish like monkfish, or cod works well)
Tinned or fresh tomatoes
100g fresh coriander

Method

1. Fry the onion, garlic, ginger and curry leaves in 2 tbsp of oil
2. In the meantime, mix all the dry spices with Tom purée and water to make a paste then add to the pan.
3. Fry for 5 mins add little water if sticking to the pan
4. Add the aubergine and cook for another 2/3 mins, then place your fish on top...I like fillet of bass... easy n tasty!!!
5. Stir occasionally, after another five minutes add the coriander n chopped tomatoes, mix well turn the hob off, and rest for 3-4 minutes
6. Serve with plain basmati rice and enjoy!

The Halstead's Satay Prawns

A Halstead favourite from their travels around the world, and seriously the best peanut sauce ever!

Ingredients - Serves 4
800g raw prawns (peeled and deveined if that's your thing)
1 tablespoon oil
¼ teaspoon chilli flakes
¼ teaspoon curry powder
¼ teaspoon salt
¼ teaspoon freshly ground black pepper

Sauce:
1 tablespoon oil
1 tablespoon finely chopped garlic
1 tablespoon finely chopped ginger
½ cup water
¼ cup peanut butter
1 tablespoon soy sauce
¼ teaspoon freshly ground black pepper
1tsp Chilli flakes
Juice of 1 lime

Method

1. Cook garlic and ginger in a pan, about 1 minute, stirring frequently.
2. Add water, peanut butter, soy sauce, pepper, and chilli until smooth. When the sauce comes to a simmer, remove it from the heat.
3. Heat oil in a pan
4. Season the prawns with the chilli, curry powder, salt, and pepper then cook on the pan (5-10 mins till cooked)
5. Before serving, reheat the sauce and add the lime juice and 2 to 3 tablespoons of water, stir to combine
6. Serve with the peanut dipping sauce.

Sam's Chicken and Prawn Gumbo

Everyone forgot to take a photo of this dish, because we dived straight in to eat, as it looked so delicious. Sam had to make it again, just to get the photo for the book, and in typical Sam-style, it's now the only professional looking photo in the book....she's such a show-off!

Ingredients - Serves 2
1 x chicken breast
1 x large onion
1 x clove of garlic
1 x green pepper
1 x celery stick
Plain flour
1 x Fresh chilli or chilli sauce
1 pint chicken stock
100g spicy/chorizo sausage
125g okra
150g raw prawns
Oil
Long Grain Rice

Method

1. Heat oil and fry onions, garlic, pepper and celery for 2 mins then add the chicken.
2. Once chicken is cooked, add approx. tablespoon of flour and stir 1 minute
3. Add chilli flakes or fresh chilli sauce to taste, along with the sausage
4. Stir in stock and cover and simmer for 20 minutes or so
5. Add okra and prawns and simmer for a further 10 minutes until cooked
6. Serve with rice

Deny's Magic Bowl
Deny makes a big comeback with an infamous Mauritian favourite!

Ingredients - Serves 4
300g Basmati rice
2 Chicken breasts cubed
200g Prawns
4 eggs
1 tbsp corn flour
200ml Water
4 cloves crushed garlic
2 tsp of fine chopped ginger
1 carrot grated
Shitaki mushrooms or button mushrooms, sliced
4 spring onions, sliced
Bunch of coriander, rough torn
Pak Choi or Chinese cabbage, sliced
454g Sweet corn
2 tbsp x Sesame oil
1x tbsp dark soy sauce
2 x tbsp light soy sauce
1 x tbsp oyster sauce
1 x tbsp rice vinegar

Method

1) Start cooking the rice according to pack instructions
2) Heat the oil in a pan and cook chicken until browned all over
3) Add the garlic, ginger, carrots, spring onions, mushrooms, pak choi, soy sauce and stir fry for a few minutes to soften the vegetables, then add the sweetcorn
4) Add the prawns, light and dark soy sauce, oyster sauce, and rice wine vinegar.
5) In a jug, stir the cornflower into 200ml water until dissolved, then add to the pan and simmer for five minutes to allow the sauce to thicken
6) In a separate pan fry the eggs
7) To serve each plate, place a fried egg in the bottom of a bowl, sunny side up, and cover with the rice/veg mix and press down to make it firm, place a plate over the top and turn it all over. Remove the bowl, and you should have a lovely mound of magic Bowl. Sprinkle with the coriander and serve!

Adam's Fried Cashew Nut with Chicken

It's a simple dish from Down Under, much like Adam ;0)

Ingredients
300g chicken
100g cashew nut or almond
70g pepper
50g large onion
2 cloves garlic
5g bell chill
1 t/b spoon of fish sauce
2 t/b spoons of oyster sauce
½ t/b spoon of sugar
3 t/b spoons of oil

Method
1. Fry the garlic until golden.
2. Add chicken, oyster sauce, fish sauce and sugar.
3. Fry until the chicken is cooked.
4. Add the cashew nuts, large pepper, large onion, and bell chilli.
5. Stir until cooked
6. Serve with rice

JPs Chicken Curry

If anyone remembers Keith Floyd's cooking programmes, it's rather like watching one of JPs demonstrations. The recipe requires a large amount of alcohol, but none of it goes in the dish! It's a mega curry though.

Ingredients for the curry - Serves 2
1 tablespoon garam masala
1 tablespoon ground cumin
½ tablespoon ground ginger
¼-1/2 tablespoon chilli powder to taste
¼ tablespoon turmeric
¼ teaspoon salt
1 tablespoon white wine vinegar
½ tablespoon oil (vegetable or ground nut preferably)
2 x breast of chicken (diced)
2 medium onions
3-4 cloves of garlic
1 x 400g tin chopped tomatoes

Ingredients for the Raita
¼ cucumber
A handful of fresh mint
1 clove garlic chopped fine
1 small tub natural yoghurt – with a few drops of lemon juice

Method for the curry

1) Mix together the curry spices with white wine vinegar, salt and oil to make a firm-ish spice paste.
2) Chop one of the onions finely and sweat off on medium heat for at least 10-15 minutes. About halfway through add the 3-4 diced cloves of garlic finely diced.
3) Add in the diced chicken and cook over a higher heat until chicken is brown,
4) Add your spice paste and cook off for a further 2-3 minutes.
5) Add 400g tin of chopped tomatoes to the mixture and bring to near boiling then reduce to a simmer (if you would like your curry hotter you can add some fresh chillies at this point).
6) Place lid on pan and cook for 15 minutes. Cut the second onion into 6-8 wedges, add to the pan and cook for a further 15 minutes. Chop a good couple of handfuls of fresh coriander and add to the curry just before serving.

Method for the Raita.

Dice the cucumber and chop the fresh mint and add the chopped garlic to the small tub of natural yoghurt.
Serve with rice of your choice and poppadum to make it even more authentic!
Enjoy

Loic's Mussels

We've been very lucky to get a Frenchman in our Kitchen (virtually of course), and experience an absolutely delicious rustic family recipe. Bon appetit, mon ami!

Ingredients - Serves 2
250gr butter
1kg mussels
3 medium sized onions diced,
1 garlic clove,
1 bunch parsley,
bay leaf,
200 gr panko breadcrumbs
10cl white wine.

Method

1) Open the mussels in a hot pan with a little white wine and bay leaf, as soon as they open, drain in a colander and keep the juices. Discard one half-shell of each mussel.

2) Sweat the onions and garlic on a low heat for around 30-45 minutes in the butter until soft and very lightly coloured.

3) Add the mussels, the breadcrumb to the pan and top up with butter and a little mussel juice.

4) Cool for a few minutes to crisp up some of the breadcrumbs, add the chopped parsley, Bon appétit!!

Matt's Well-Hot Easy Prawn Burgers

Matt made up this vague recipe from memories of something he ate in a pub once. I'm surprised Matt remembers anything after being in a pub.

"some" cabbage

Burger Ingredients - Serves 4
720g Raw Prawns, shells off and deveined
1 egg
1 red chilli, finely chopped (seeds in or out depending how much heat you like)
2 tsp cornflower
200g breadcrumbs
Sunflower oil for frying

Asian-ish style slaw ingredients
Matt was quite vague on the quantity of cabbage required...when pressed on the subject, he said "depends how much you want".... cheers Matt!
Some sliced white cabbage (probably half...maybe)
Some sliced red cabbage (could be half....maybe)
Juice and zest of a lime
1 grated carrot
A good glug of sesame oil

Other things
Burger buns – brioche works well
Some Mayo (probably a good squirt on each burger?)
Some Sweet Chilli sauce (maybe a drizzle on each...possibly?)
1 red chilli chopped

Method
1) Make 3 piles of prawns. Chop one pile fine, chop one pile into slices, and chop the last pile into of prawns into thirds
2) Mix the prawns with the egg white, chilli and breadcrumbs until the mixture can hold it's shape
3) Divide the mixture into four balls and shape into burgers and put in the fridge while you make the slaw
4) Making the slaw involves slicing, grating and tossing the ingredients in a bowl
5) Take the burgers out of the fridge, and fry them both sides until golden brown
6) Serve in the buns, with the mayo, sweet chilli sauce and "some" slaw

Mr B's Jamaican Jerk Tuna Curry

Big flavours and slightly different twist on the traditional jerk curry, with the addition of slow cooked onions.

Ingredients for the sauce – serves 4

2 Scotch Bonnet peppers chopped
1 small red onion chopped
3 garlic cloves chopped
2 spring onions
1tbsp soy sauce
1tbsp vinegar (use white vinegar or apple cider vinegar to your preference)
1 tbsp olive oil
Juice from 1/2 orange
Juice from half a lime
1tsp freshly grated ginger
2tsp brown sugar
1 tsp nutmeg
1 tsp allspice
1 tsp cinnamon
1 tsp dried thyme
Salt and pepper

Other ingredients
1 large red onion, sliced
100g butter
2 tuna steaks or chicken breasts, cut into bitesize cubes
2 black plantain, cut into diagonal slices
200g Basmati rice
Tin of kidney beans
2 red onions
Cooking oil

Equipment
2 frying pans
Rice cooker/pan
Blender

Method
1) Put all the sauce ingredients in a blender, and whizz up until smooth
2) Fry the red onion, low and slow in the butter for about 40 mins until softened and very lightly coloured, then removed from pan
3) Fry tuna or chicken until browned
4) Add the fried onions and sauce, then turn down to a low simmer for 20 mins
5) Cook your rice according to the pack instructions and heat up the kidney beans
6) Fry the sliced plantain until lightly browned both sides
7) Drain the cooked rice and kidney beans, then stir together to create the "rice'n'peas"
8) To plate up, serve a few of the plantain, with a couple of big spoonful of rice'n'peas, and the Jerk Curry. Irie!

Loic's Fish Tagine
The Frenchman makes an encore with this simple quick and tasty recipe...vivre la jour!

Ingredients - Serves 2
450g firm white fish (i.e. cod, monkfish, haddock), cut into 5cm cubes
2 Tbsp olive oil, plus extra for brushing
3 celery sticks, chopped
2 carrot, chopped
1 fennel, chopped
1 small onion, chopped
1 preserved lemon, finely chopped
4 plum tomatoes, sliced, seeds out
600ml/1 pint fish stock
8 small new potatoes, cut lengthways into quarters
salt and freshly ground black pepper
Cous Cous for two

For the chermoula:
2 Tbsp roughly chopped fresh coriander
3 garlic cloves, chopped
1 1/2 tsp ground cumin
1/2 red finger chilli, seeded and chopped roughly
1/2 tsp saffron strands
4 Tbsp extra virgin olive oil

1 lemon, juice only
1 1/2 tsp paprika
1 tsp salt

Method

1) Blend all the chermoula ingredients together in a blender. Heat 1 tbsp of oil in a pan and add the blended chermoula and fry for a couple of minutes
2) Add the onion, carrot, celery and fennel and fry gently until softened
3) Add the tomatoes, lemons, stock and potatoes to the pan, turn up the heat to almost a boil, then reduce to a simmer
4) When the potatoes are softened, add the fish to the pan and continue to simmer until the fish is cooked through
5) Serve with cous cous

The Bowden's Thai Salad

Very fresh and zingy flavours from this super healthy dish, made up from a vague recollection of something eaten on a distant holiday.

Ingredients – Serves 4
250g Chicken cut into cubes
200g Cooked King Prawns
1 Cucumber chopped into 1cm cubes
250g Cherry Tomatoes halved
5cm Ginger finely chopped
4 Cloves of Garlic finely chopped
2 Sticks of Lemongrass finely chopped
2 Red Chillies finely chopped (seeds out if you don't like a lot of heat)
500g Fine Rice Noodles (cooked)
200g Fresh Coriander torn into rough pieces
1 lime zest and juice
4 tsp Thai Seven Spice
1 Tbsp Fish Sauce
1 tbsp sunflower oil

Equipment: Wok, Large Serving Bowl

Method

1) Put the halved cherry tomatoes and chopped cucumber, ginger, garlic, lemongrass, chillies and coriander into the large serving bowl
2) Pour over the lime zest and juice and fish sauce, and give it all a good toss
3) Heat the sunflower oil in a wok, add the chopped chicken, and stir fry until golden all sides
4) Keep frying the chicken until it's cooked through, then add the king prawns and fry for another minute
5) Add the Thai seven spice and turn the chicken until well coated
6) Add the cooked rice noodles and stir fry for another minute until warmed through, and coated in the spice
7) Add the contents of the wok to the serving bowl and give all the ingredients another good toss....and serve!

Salmon a-la-Blanco

A very fresh and tasty dish. Whilst the salmon was cooking Martin gave us an 'interesting' trumpet recital which several of his neighbours were able to experience what we'll call 'the noise' as well.

Ingredients – serves 2
200g long grain rice
200ml coconut milk
2 x Salmon fillet
Half mango, diced

For the salsa
1/4 fresh pineapple
1 Avocado, diced
100g fresh coriander, chopped
1 red onion, diced
1 tomato, seeds/water removed, flesh diced
1 red chilli, chopped fine
1 lime, juiced

Method

Pre-heat the oven to 180c

1. Place the salmon fillets on a greased baking tray and drizzle with olive oil
2. Cook in the oven for 8-10 minutes
3. Meanwhile cook the rice with the coconut milk
4. Toss the salsa ingredients in a bowl and season with the lime juice
5. Place the cooked salmon onto your serving plate and serve with timbals of salsa, and coconut rice

Lilly P's Stir Fry (age 13)

Small twit, Lilly P, gave us an excellent demo and very tasty Friday night Chinese.

Ingredients – serves 4
225g Medium Egg Noodles
3 litres boiling water
1 ½ tsp salt
1 tsp sesame oil
250ml water
2 tsp cornflour
1 tbsp soy sauce
1 chicken or veg stock cube
1 tbsp cooking oil
1 ½ cups finely chopped cabbage
1 medium onion thinly sliced
1 medium carrot grated
1 red chilli, seeds and ribs removed
1 cup freshly sliced white mushrooms
170g mange tout
Salt and pepper according to taste

Method

1. Cook noodles in the boiling water with 1 tsp of salt for indicated time on packet. Stirring occasionally until al denté (tender but firm). Drain and return to the same pot.
2. Add sesame oil to the noodles, stir through and cover the noodles to keep warm.
3. Stir your water into your cornflour in a small bowl until smooth. Stir in soy sauce and stock powder and set aside.
4. Heat wok or large frying pan until very hot. Add cooking oil. Then add in the cabbage, onion and grated carrot. Stir for about 3 minutes until vegetables are tender but firm.
5. Add the capsicum, mushroom and snow peas with some seasoning. Stir-fry for about 2-3 minutes until the pepper and snow peas are tender but have a slight crunch to them.
6. Give the cornflour one last stir and slowly add it to the vegetables, stirring constantly until boiling and thickened.
7. Add the noodles and stir for 1-2 minutes until fully heated through

Hugh's Awful Noodle Thing

Also known as 'Hugh & Lind's Vietnamese Beef Noodle Soup'. Hugh's not happy unless he's being horrible about your stuff, so I've renamed it for him. It's actually quite good.....but don't tell him.

Stock ingredients:* - Serves 6

2 onions
2 carrots
3 inches fresh ginger
6 cloves
6 Star anise
2 sticks cinnamon
1 tsp black peppercorns
2 tbsp soy sauce
3 tbsp fish sauce
1kg beef shank or brisket
1 beef stock cube

Other ingredients:
250g sirloin steak
500g rice stick noodles
1 onion
6 spring onions
2 red chilis
Half cup beansprouts
Bunch of coriander and mint
2 limes
Hoisin & Soy sauce

Method
Make the stock first.
1) Put all the ingredients (except the fish sauce) in a big pan with 5 pints water.
2) Bring to the boil and then simmer with lid on for an hour, skimming off any fat as it appears.
3) Remove lid and simmer until stock reduced to about 3 pints.
4) Strain stock into another pan so you are left with just liquid.

If you haven't time to make the stock from scratch you can cheat… you can either buy pots of quality beef stock (3 pints worth) and add the other stock ingredients to this, leaving out the beef brisket and stock cube. Or you can really cheat and get a pot of Pho paste. Just make up 3 pints of the stock according to directions.

Now time to get chopping.
1) Cut the sirloin really thinly against the grain and the onions, spring onions and chillies really finely. Chop coriander and mint (leaves only).
2) Bring stock up to the boil and add fish sauce and season with salt and pepper to taste. Reduce heat and leave simmering until ready to use.

3) Cook your noodles in boiling water according to instructions and divide between 6 bowls. Top each with sirloin steak, onions, spring onions, chilis (amounts according to your taste).

Ladle over the hot stock and top with beansprouts and chopped herbs. Serve with lime wedges, hoisin, soy and fish sauce – add to your taste.

Andy's Wild Forest Mushrooms and Chorizo

Andy managed to entertain us this evening without breaking any bones, which is quite an achievement for Andy

Ingredients – serves 2
300g wild forest mushrooms (also goes well with chicken, salmon or cod)
300g of cherry or baby plum tomatoes, halved
4 sprigs of fresh basil
8 black olives finely chopped
100g of Chorizo cut into small cubes
1 tbsp red wine vinegar
Salt
Black pepper
2 tbsp olive oil
Cous Cous or basmati rice for two

Method

1. In a bowl gently stir together the cherry tomatoes, basil leaves, chopped olives, 1 tbsp olive oil and red wine vinegar. Season with a pinch of salt and black pepper.
2. Heat 1 tbsp oil in a pan and add the mushrooms and fry for 5 minutes
3. Add the chorizo to the pan and fry for a further 2 minutes
4. Add the tomato mixture and fry for 30 seconds.
5. Serve on a bed of cous cous or basmati rice

Lyndon's Spicy Spanish Paella

Senior Lyndon came out all guns blazing for his demonstration, strangely dressing as a Mexican bandit for the occasion....he poco loco!

45 min cooking time
Paella pan or 2 large frying pans
Blender – "We use a Nutribullit" (lah-de-dah Lyndon!!)

Ingredients - Serves 4
Olive oil
Salt & Pepper
Paella rice 500g
Bread (Bagutte or a fresh cob)
Lemons x 4
1 litre of Chicken stock
2 Spicy chorizo cut into lardon size pieces
1 chicken breast cut into bite size chunks
500g a bag of defrosted mixed sea food selection
1 cup of frozen peas
Parsley
Salt & Pepper

Sauce (Sofrito) Ingredients
Saffron a large pinch
2 tsp Paprika
2 tsp Smoked Paprika
2 tsp Dried Thyme
4 Medium tomatoes
4 Sweet Piquante peppers
4 cloves of garlic
Olive oil

Method
1) Put all the sofrito ingredients in a blender and whizz until smooth, then set aside
2) Warm the oil in a paella pan over a medium heat, add the chicken and fry until sealed all sides (turns white), about a minute, then remove from the pan
3) Put the rice into the pan and stir to coat it with the oil
4) Add the Sofrito to the rice and stir well, bringing it to a simmer
5) Add the chicken pieces back to the pan
6) Slowly add the chicken stock and saffron, combining it well as you go, keeping the simmer going
7) Add the peas and salt & pepper to taste
8) Keep stirring to prevent it sticking until the rice becomes al-dente, if it starts to dry out add a bit of water just to keep it loose, but not runny!
9) Add the seafood and cover with foil for about 5 minutes until it's cooked
10) Serve with lemon wedges

Tristan's Salmon Pancake Rolls (age 11)

A favourite in Tristan's house for family movie nights.

Ingredients - serves 4
24 Frozen Pancakes for Crispy Duck (from Asian shops) - defrosted
600g of salmon fillet or chicken strips
Cucumber cut into skinny batons
Bunch of coriander, rough torn
Good quality tahini humous (Sabra brand is best)
2-3 tsp Thai Seven Spice
1 Lime
Oven to 200c or fan 180c before we start

Method
1) Oil a baking tray and bake the salmon or chicken strips for 20 minutes until cooked through
2) Squeeze the juice of one lime onto the meat and sprinkle over the Thai Seven Spice until lightly coated all sides, pop back in the oven for 5 minutes
3) Remove the meat from the oven and put in a bowl, the salmon can be roughly flaked in the bowl
4) To serve, take a pancake, smear a teaspoon of hummus on it. Then add a pinch of the cucumber and coriander, roll the pancake and enjoy!

B's Manakeesh with Mushrooms, Feta, Onion and Olives
A very easy and tasty Lebanese recipe

Dough Ingredients – makes 8 breads
3 cups Bread Flour
7g Active Dry Yeast
1 tsp Sugar
1 cup luke warm water
⅓ cup Vegetable Oil
1 tsp Salt

Topping
12 tbsp Za'atar
12 tbsp. Olive Oil
200g Feta cheese, rough crumbled
200g sliced mushrooms
1 white onion, sliced fine
100g sliced black olives

Method
1) In a large bowl combine the yeast, sugar and ½ cup of the warm water. Mix together and set aside for about 10 minutes until a foam forms on the surface.
2) Add the flour and stir with a wooden spoon to combine.
3) Slowly add the oil while stirring to combine evenly with the dough.

4) Cover the bowl with a kitchen towel and place somewhere warm to rise….it should end up about double the size.
5) Fry the mushrooms until they're soft and rubbery, then set aside
6) Take the dough out of the bowl with floured hands and make a large ball. Then divide the dough into 8 balls, and roll the balls out into flat breads with a rolling pin on a floured surface…about 6 inches diameter
7) Combine the za'atar and olive oil in a small bowl, then spread evenly over the breads, leaving a 1cm edge of dough
8) Top with the mushrooms, crumbled feta, onion slices and olives
9) Pop in the oven at 200c and bake for 20 mins until the edges are golden brown

Ridley's Seafood Chowder with No-Knead Bread (age 14)

A recipe handed down by the Old Foss (a salty sea dog),
made up for lunch on a cold day fishing on the Solent.

Ingredients - Serves 4

For the Bread
1 sachet fast action yeast
1tsp salt
1 tsp sugar
500g bread flour

For the Chowder
500g Fish Pie Mix (Salmon, Cod, Smoked Haddock)
200g prawns
3/4 pint fish stock
1 big onion
4 cloves garlic
2 pints whole milk
285g tin of sweetcorn
1 cup of rice
1 glass of wine
2 tsp black pepper
2 tsp paprika
2 tsp ground cumin
1 tsp salt (or to taste)

Equipment

For the bread....large bowl, baking tray and baking paper

For the chowder...a big heavy bottom pan

Method

1) Sweat onion and garlic until soft
2) Add wine nd reduce for 5 mins
3) Add rice, pepper, stock, cumin and paprika
4) When rice is soft, add sweetcorn, fish and milk
5) Simmer until fish is cooked
6) Remove half the soup to a blender and add prawns to the remaining pan
7) Blitz the other half and return to the pan
8) Serve with the bread

Johnny's Asian Happy Ending
The long awaited and highly anticipated demonstration
from Johnny....a lovely way to end the week!

Ingredients - serves 4
300g pre-cooked fine rice noodles
Olive / rapeseed oil, for frying
2 medium white onions, sliced very fine
1 red pepper, medium slices
2 parsnips, grated
1 savoy cabbage, medium sliced
1 chilli, chopped
4 garlic cloves fine chopped
4 teaspoons madras curry powder
1 tsp dried chilli flakes
Bunch of spring onions, chopped
2 tbsp light soy sauce
1 tbsp sesame oil

Method

1) Stir-fry the parsnip, onion, pepper and chilli until softened (about 10 mins)
2) Add the garlic, cabbage, noodles and spring onion, curry powder, chilli flakes, soy sauce and sesame oil
3) Combine well, heat through and serve

Hugh's Fat Boy Friday Kofte

Hugh's back with another terrible demonstration of this delicious recipe, improved by the assistance of his far more sensible daughter.

Ingredients for the Kofte – serves 4
500g lamb mince
2 teaspoons of thyme (fresh or dried))
Chilli flakes/powder to taste (a tablespoon will prob. blow your head off – so 2 teaspoonfuls...?)
Tablespoon of ground cumin
1 tablespoon of sumac (or the grated zest of a lemon) – but sumac is better if you can get it (cos its Turkish)
Salt n pepper

The garnish
Half an iceberg lettuce (shredded)
Red onion (which we are going to slice very, very, very thinly
Mr Hazell)
A lemon
Bunch of flat leaf parsley, chopped

Heidi's Tzatziki
250g natural or greek yoghurt
Half a cucumber grated (cut in half lengthways and scrape
out the watery seeds first)
Handful of mint, finely chopped
2 garlic cloves, crushed
The juice of a lovely lemon
A glug of Olive oil

E Z Flatbread
250g self raising flour
250g natural or greek yoghurt

Equipment you'll need
A mixing bowl, frying pan and rolling pin for the flatbreads
A big mixing bowl, hands, hot oven, and baking tray for the
kofta
A mixing bowl, grater, chopping board for tzatziki

Method
1) Warm the oven to 200c/180c fan
2) To make the koftes, mix all the kofte ingredients
   together in a bowl and form sausage shapes with the
   mix. You should end up with 8 large ones, or 16 small
   ones. Wet hands help to stop them sticking to you
3) To make the Tzatziki, stir all those ingredients
   together as well in a separate clean bowl
4) Garnish – slice the red onion into very fine slices,
   place in a bowl, squeeze over the juice of the lemon,
   and sprinkle over the parsley. Cut the lettuce into
   1cm slices and put that in another bowl.

5) To make the flatbread, stir the flour and yogurt together to form a soft smooth dough, them separate into eight even sized balls. The easiest way to do this is make a large ball first, then cut, like an orange, into eight segments). Then roll them out with a floured rolling pin to make 8 flat breads about 6 inches diameter
6) Put your koftes in the oven on a greased baking tray for 20-30 mins until cooked through
7) While the koftes are cooking, cook the flat breads, one by one in a frying pan…..you can use a dry pan, or a teaspoon of oil for each. Both ways cook until the breads puff and brown when cooked both sides….if you use oil, they'll also be slightly crispy.

To serve, smear a dessertspoon of tzatziki over a flatbread, pop in a kofte, garnish with the onions and lettuce, fold and eat!!

Some Desserts

Gigi's Vanilla Pancakes (age 10)
This is Gigi's adaption her grandma's family pancake recipe which has been caressed down through the mists of time.
Good work Gigi!

Ingredients - Serves 4

- 2 cups self-raising flour
- 1 egg
- 2 cup milk
- 1 tsp cinnamon
- 1 tsp vanilla essence

Toppings: lemon, sugar, ice cream, chocolate sauce, Nutella, compote, maple syrup….

Method

1. Sift flour into a bowl
2. Mix whisked egg into flour
3. Then while stirring pour in milk slowly
4. Add vanilla essence and cinnamon
5. Stir well (use a mixer to make this really smooth)
6. Heat pan, melt butter
7. Then cook pancakes one at a time, 46pprox.. 1 ladle per pancake, over a high heat
8. As you cook, put cooked pancakes in oven (low temp) to keep warm
9. Add toppings
10. Eat!

Will's Honeycomb Cheesecake (age 14)
Amazingly delicious cheesecake expertly demonstrated by you Will. Have some insulin standing by though!

Ingredients
250g crushed digestive biscuits
100g salted butter
½ teaspoon Vanilla extract
600g full fat cream-cheese
100g icing sugar
284 ml of double cream
1/2 lemon juiced
3 crunchies
25cm cake tin with loose base

Method
1) Melt the butter and mix with the crushed biscuits.
2) Press into the cake tin and put in the fridge for 30 mins.
3) Mix the rest of the ingredients in a bowl until smooth and fold in two broken crunchies
4) Spoon the filling onto the biscuit base
5) Put back in the fridge to set for an hour.
6) Sprinkle the remaining broken crunchie on top

Sarah's Super Salted Caramel Profiteroles

Sarah held back from demonstrating a recipe until near the end of lockdown then dropped this bomb...Profiterole heaven!

Ingredients for 16 profiteroles – serves 4

For the Choux
150 ml water
55g butter
70g plain flour
2 beaten eggs
(Will need mixing, piping, cooking & cooling so ensure you have a pan, spatula, piping bag, baking tray, cooling rack & grease proof paper)

For the filling
500ml double cream (will need to be beaten so ensure you have a whisk or similar)
2 tablespoons icing sugar (not essential)

For the topping:
100g butter
4 tablespoons soft brown light sugar (or similar)
4 tablespoons caster sugar
4 tablespoons double cream
Up to 1 teaspoon sea salt, to taste

Method
The Choux Pastry

1) Get all your ingredients and equipment ready as things happen quickly!
2) Turn oven on to 200c
3) Heat the water and butter in a pan over a medium heat until the butter has melted into the water, keep stirring to mix it well
4) When the butter has melted, remove from the heat and stir in the flour to make a golden dough
5) Turn the dough out onto the baking paper and spread out with a spatula to cool quickly on a wire tray
6) Once the dough has cooled to a tepid feel, put back in the pan (no heat!) and gradually stir in the eggs to make a dough paste that you'll be able to pipe.
7) Put your baking paper on a baking tray, and pipe on the dough paste to make 16 balls, smooth any peaks so they don't burn
8) Pop in the oven until golden brown (about 20 minutes)
9) Remove from the oven and make a hole in the bottom of each (the end of a chopstick is about right) to let the steam out, and place on a cooling rack.

The Filling
Whip the double cream until it makes standing peaks (with the icing sugar if being used)

The Topping

Put all the ingredients in a pan over a medium/high heat and keep stirring until mixed well and you no longer feel the grains of sugar and remove from the heat.

To Serve

1) When the pastry balls have cooled, pipe the cream into them through the hole your made earlier
2) Arrange in a dish and pour the topping all over

Laura's Luscious Lemon Syllabub

This tasty dish is sweet and simple, the syllabub that is not Laura...well maybe, you'd better ask her husband.

This quick and rather indulgent dessert is so quick and easy to make and can be made ahead of time.

Ingredients - Serves 6
4oz of caster sugar
4 tablespoons of Sherry or limoncello
1 whole lemon (zest and juice)
1/2 pint of double cream
Fresh raspberries

Equipment
Electric whisk
Large bowl
Measuring jug

Method

1. Place the double cream and sugar in a large mixing bowl
2. Zest and juice the lemon and add to the other ingredients in the bowl
3. Add the sherry or limoncello to the bowl and whisk all the ingredients together with an electric whisk. Be sure to whisk carefully as you want the mixture to be well combined, lovely and smooth but not stodgy, and not so long it turns into cottage cheese like JP's did!!!
4. Put the mixture in one large serving bowl or divide into 6 individual dishes.
5. Place in the fridge until ready to serve.
6. Garnish with raspberries before eating.

A couple of cakes

Heidi's Lemon Drizzle Cake (age 13)

Heidi was just as surprised as the rest of us that this turned out ok. More than just ok, in fact the best lemon drizzle cake any of us had eaten. Well done Heidels!

Ingredients
150g butter
150g caster sugar
150g SR flour
Zest of 2 large lemons
3 large eggs
2 tbsp milk
1 tsp vanilla extract
Icing sugar to dust
Lemon slices/peel and grated carrot for decoration
Syrup: 100g icing sugar, juice of your 2 lemons

Method

Heat the oven to 190 or 175 fan

1) Grease and line a loaf tin or me any medium sized tin
2) Whisk butter, sugar & zest together
3) Add beaten eggs slowly, whisking as you go.
4) Add sifted flour gradually, whisking as you go.
5) Stir in milk and vanilla extract
6) Pop into tin and bake for 40 mins.
7) Remove from oven but leave cake in tin and place on wire rack.
8) Make the syrup by putting icing sugar and lemon juice in a pan,
9) Use fork to prick the warm cake and pour over syrup and leave to cool.
10) Turn out onto serving plate pour over the syrup and decorate with lemon slices/peel and a little grated carrot.

Mr B's Carrot Cake

I've tried a few carrot cakes in my time, but this recipe makes the best ever!

Ingredients for the Carrot Cake:

3 eggs
150g vegetable oil
400g granulated sugar
300g self-raising flour
2 tsp baking powder
1 tsp bicarbonate of soda
1/2 tsp salt
1 tsp ground cinnamon
225g freshly grated carrots
435g tin of crushed pineapple lightly drained
75g desiccated coconut
A handful of pecans
A handful of sultanas

Ingredients for the Frosting:
227g softened cream cheese
100g unsalted butter softened
1 tsp vanilla essence
360g icing sugar
Pinch of salt

Method
Preheat the oven 180° C
Make the batter
1. Whisk together the eggs, oil, and sugar.
2. Stir in the flour, baking powder, baking soda, salt, and cinnamon.
3. Fold in the carrots, coconut, and pineapple (and nuts and raisins if using)
4. Pour the batter into a couple of sandwich cake tins
5. Bake in the oven until golden brown, about 40 minutes.
6. Allow the cake to cool completely

Make the frosting
1. Beat the softened cream cheese together with the softened butter with a hand mixer until smooth, about 2 minutes.
2. Add the icing sugar, vanilla, and pinch of salt. Mix on low for 30 seconds, then turn to medium- high and beat for 3 minutes until smooth and creamy. Add a little more sugar if it's too loose or a little milk if it's too thick.
3. When the cake is completely cooled, fill and frost the cake
4. Decorate with some glazed grated carrot

A Couple Of 'Strong' Cocktails

The Perfect Singapore Sling
This pre-dinner cocktail made the perfect accompaniment to Johnny's Asian Happy Ending...really rather good!

Ingredients
25ml dry gin
25ml cherry brandy
25ml Benedictine
handful of ice, to serve
few drops Angostura bitters
50ml pineapple juice
25ml lime juice
sparkling water to top up
For the garnish
1 thin slice of fresh pineapple (optional)
cocktail cherry

Method

STEP 1

Pour the gin, cherry brandy and Benedictine into a mixing glass or a jug. Add the ice and Angostura bitters. Stir well until the outside of the glass feels cold.

STEP 2

Pour the mix into a tall glass, then add the pineapple juice and lime juice and stir gently. Top up with sparkling water and garnish.

Vespers

"I never have more than one drink before dinner. But I do like that one to be large and very strong and very cold, and very well-made" – James Bond

We did a 007 themed online fancy dress party one Friday and, of course, there was only one drink to have!

Ingredients
Three measures of Gin
One measure of Vodka
Half a measure of Lillet
Handful of ice
Lemon peel

Method
1) Put all the alcohol ingredients into a cocktail shaker, with the ice
2) Shake it very well until it's ice-cold (shaken, not stirred!!)
3) Pour into a cocktail glass and add a large thin slice of lemon peel

Very important to drink quite quickly while it's ice cold!

Printed in Great Britain
by Amazon